THE TRUTH ABOUT

THE LAST DAYS' TEMPLE

THOMAS ICE AND TIMOTHY DEMY

HARVEST HOUSE PUBLISHERS
Eugene, Oregon 97402

Scripture quotations are taken from the New American Standard Bible, © 1960, 1962, 1963, 1968, 1971, 1972, 1973, 1975, 1977 by The Lockman Foundation. Used by permission.

All views expressed are solely the individual authors' and do not reflect the position of any governmental agency or department.

Cover by Left Coast Design, Portland, Oregon

THE TRUTH ABOUT THE LAST DAYS' TEMPLE

Copyright © 1996 by Pre-Trib Research Center
Published by Harvest House Publishers
Eugene, Oregon 97402

ISBN 1-56507-393-2

All rights reserved. No portion of this book may be reproduced in any form without the written permission of the Publisher.

Printed in the United States of America.

98 99 00 01 02 03 / BF / 11 10 9 8 7 6 5 4 3

Contents

P A R T 4

What Else Do We Know About
the Millennial Temple?

P A R T 5

What Is the Significance
of the Temples for Christians Today?

About this series...

The Pocket Prophecy series is designed to provide readers with a brief summary of individual topics and issues in Bible prophecy. For quick reference and ease in studying, the works are written in a question-and-answer format. The questions follow a logical progression so that people who read straight through will receive a greater appreciation for the topic and the issues involved. Each issue is fully documented and contains a bibliography of recommended reading for those people who desire to pursue their study in greater depth.

The theological perspective presented throughout the series is that of premillennialism and pretribulationism. The authors recognize that this is not the only position embraced by evangelical Christians, but we believe that it is the most widely held and prominent perspective. It is also our conviction that premillennialism and, specifically, pretribulationism, best explains the prophetic plan of God as revealed in the Bible.

The study of prophecy and its puzzling pieces is an endeavor which is detailed and complex—but not beyond comprehension or resolution. It is open to error, misinterpretation, and confusion. Such possibilities should not, however, cause any Christian to shy away from either the study of prophecy or engagement in honest and helpful discussions about it. The goal of this series is to provide all those who desire to better understand the Scriptures with a concise and consistent tool. If you will do the digging, the rewards will be great and the satisfaction will remain with you as you grow in your knowledge and love of our Lord Jesus Christ and His Word.

PART 1

What Is
the Last Days' Temple?

In 1989, *Time* magazine published an article entitled "Time for a New Temple?" in which it reported the growing desire of many devout Jews to see a new Temple constructed on the Temple Mount in Jerusalem. The correspondent began by writing:

> "May it be Thy will that the Temple be speedily rebuilt in our days...." That plea to God, recited three times a day in Jewish prayers, expresses a yearning that makes Jerusalem's Temple Mount potentially the most volatile 35 acres on earth.[1]

In the years since that article, nothing has diminished the desire for the rebuilding of the Temple. In fact, the anticipation and preparation continues to grow. Israeli public support for a rebuilt Temple, once low, is steadily increasing. Tensions in the Middle East remain high and the region's religious and political problems continue to make headlines in the news around the world. Yet, even in these turbulent times, Temple Movement activists continue to intensify their efforts.

The forces of politics, diplomacy, religion, and culture all converge on the Temple Mount—arguably the most significant real estate on earth. One major conflict between the Jews and Muslims is that a Muslim mosque, the Dome of the Rock, is built on top of what is generally recognized as the site of the Jerusalem Temple. Temple activism has provoked international concern and conflict, and remains a short fuse which could ignite the next world war. There are no easy or simple solutions in this complex international drama and rhetoric runs high.

The leader of the Temple Mount Faithful, Dr. Gershon Salomon, who is one of the most visible and vocal advocates for a rebuilt Temple, declares:

> I believe this is the will of God. It [the Dome of the Rock] must be moved. We must, you know, take it from the place. And today we have all the instruments to do it, stone by stone, very carefully, and then put it in a package and mail it back to Mecca, the place from where it was brought.[2]

Statements such as the one above are highly charged with emotion and held with firm conviction. Any activity surrounding the Temple Mount is certain to foster chaos and draw condemnation from one or more of the religious or political entities involved.

Yet, the dream of rebuilding the Temple is both realistic and biblically accurate; it will one day be fully realized. *The Bible explicitly teaches that rebuilding will become a reality.* However, the joy will be fleeting and the worship will be interrupted. As we will see from glimpses of history and the Bible, the new Temple will be neither the first nor the last to be erected. Its construction is certain, but so are the turbulent days that will accompany it.

1. How many Temples are mentioned in the Bible?

The Bible uses the term *temple* in many ways. The English word temple is derived from the Latin term *templum*, which is a translation of the Hebrew noun *hekal*, meaning "big house." In the Old Testament, temple almost always refers to the Jerusalem Temple. As we move into the New Testament, the primary use of temple remains the Jerusalem Temple. However, Christ compared His body to that Temple (see Matthew 26: 61; Mark 14:58; 15:29; John 2:19). The apostle Paul speaks of the "body of Christ" as a spiritual temple (Ephesians 2:21); and the body of the individual believer as a "temple of the Holy Spirit": "Do you not know that you are a temple of God, and that the Spirit of God dwells in you?" (1 Corinthians 3:16; see also 6:19).

The Bible, at times, also speaks of a heavenly Temple. Isaiah was caught up to heaven and describes a scene that could well be the heavenly Temple (Isaiah 6). John, the Revelator, having been caught up into heaven, specifically speaks of a heavenly Temple from where God oversees the judgments of the tribulation and sends forth His angels at His command (Revelation 7:15; 11:19; 14:15,17; 15:5,6,8; 16:1,17). The heavenly Temple, in some sense, serves as a model for the various earthly dwellings of God (i.e., the Tabernacle, Temple, and spiritual Temple).

In relation to the Temple in Jerusalem, the Bible speaks of four other Temples.

> Four Jerusalem Temples are mentioned in the Bible. Two (Solomon's and Herod's) have come and gone, but two more (the Tribulation Temple and the Millennial Temple) are prophesied to be built in the future. The final Temple (Millennial) will be erected by the Lord Jesus Christ Himself when He establishes the Messianic kingdom.... But the Tribulation Temple must come first.[3]

It is noteworthy that in eternity there is no temple.

"[An angel] showed me the holy city, Jerusalem, coming down out of heaven from God.... And I saw no temple in it, for the Lord God, the Almighty, and the Lamb, are its temple" (Revelation 21:10,22).

2. How did the Tabernacle prepare Israel for the Temple?

The Tabernacle could be viewed as a "mobile Temple"—a transient Temple for a transient people. "The Tabernacle was a temporary structure, moving from place to place until the Israelites were unified politically and spiritually."[4] As a precursor to Solomon's Temple, the Tabernacle served many of the same functions and purposes.

Israel became a nation upon their deliverance from slavery in Egypt. At this point, God's presence was manifested through a cloud by day and a fiery pillar by night. Once the Israelites were free from Pharaoh's pursuit, the Lord instructed them concerning the Tabernacle's construction:

> And let them construct a sanctuary for Me, that I may dwell among them. According to all that I am going to show you, as the pattern of the tabernacle and the pattern of all its furniture, just so you shall construct it (Exodus 25:8,9).

The Four Jerusalem Temples of Israel

First Temple (Solomon's)
Shekinah present
(1 Kings 5–8)

Second Temple (Zerubbabel's & Herod's)
Roman eagle present
(Ezra 3:7–6:18; Matt. 24:1-2; Mark 13:1-2; Luke 21:5-6)

Messiah's First Coming

Temple in Ruins
Dome of the Rock dominates site
Jewish Diaspora Church Age
Gentile inclusion (Rom. 9–11)

Third Temple
Abomination of Desolation present
(2 Thess. 2:4; Rev. 11:1-2)

Messiah's Second Coming

Millennial Temple
Shekinah present
(Ezek. 40–43:27; Isa. 2:2-3; 56:7)

374 Years | 70 Years | 586 Years | 7 Years | 1,000 Years

960 B.C. — First Temple Built

586 B.C. — First Temple Destroyed (by Babylonians)

516 B.C. — Second Temple Built (Zerubbabel's)

19 B.C. — Second Temple Enlarged (Herod's)

A.D. 70 — Second Temple Destroyed (by Romans)

The Church Christ's Spiritual Temple (Acts 2; Eph. 2)

Third Temple Built

Battle of Gog & Magog (Ezek. 38–39)

Third Temple desecrated (by Antichrist) (Dan. 9:26-27; 11:31; 12:11; Matt. 24:15; Mark 13:14)

Millennium (Messianic Age) (Isa. 2:2-4; 11; 29:6; Ps. 2; Dan. 7:13-14; Jer. 23:5; Zech. 14:9-21; Matt. 19:28; Acts 1:6-7; 3:18-24; Rom. 8:18-22; Heb. 2:10; Rev. 11:5; 20)

Fourth Temple Built (by Messiah)

> And I will consecrate the tent of meeting and the altar; I
> will also consecrate Aaron and his sons to minister as
> priests to Me. And I will dwell among the sons of Israel
> and will be their God. And they shall know that I am the
> LORD their God who brought them out of the land of
> Egypt, that I might dwell among them; I am the LORD
> their God (Exodus 29:44-46).

Even while Israel was in her wilderness sojourn, God prepared for a future time when the Tabernacle would become the
Temple.

> But you shall seek the LORD at the place which the LORD
> your God shall choose from all your tribes, to establish
> His name there for His dwelling, and there you shall
> come.... When you cross the Jordan and live in the land
> which the LORD your God is giving you to inherit, and He
> gives you rest from all your enemies around you so that
> you live in security, then it shall come about that the place
> in which the LORD your God shall choose for His name to
> dwell, there you shall bring all that I command you: your
> burnt offerings and your sacrifices, your tithes and the
> contribution of your hand, and all your choice votive
> offerings which you will vow to the LORD (Deuteronomy
> 12:5,10,11).

After the nation entered the Promised Land, and David
became king, God spoke with him about the building of the
Temple. David's dream became Solomon's reality. Once the
Temple was consecrated, God's visible presence shifted from
the Tabernacle to the Temple. "I have chosen and consecrated
this house that My name may be there forever, and My eyes and
My heart will be there perpetually" (2 Chronicles 7:16).

The temporary Tabernacle prepared the way for the permanent Temple by establishing the pattern and purpose for Israel's
worship of the Lord. Once Israel moved from the Tabernacle to
the Temple, the site of God's presence became set and sacred for
the remainder of history.

3. What is the purpose of Israel's Temple?

Israel's Temple provided God's people with a visible symbol
of His invisible presence and served to teach the Jews many

lessons. Even though Israel was like the Gentiles in that all had temples relating to their gods, Israel's Temple was different in 'many ways:

> Throughout the ancient Near East, temples were built as royal residences for the gods of the people. Man's duty was to provide for the physical needs of the gods: food, water, clothing, and innumerable delicacies, and in exchange for these services, the gods were expected to provide human necessities.
>
> Israelite worship stood in opposition to this pagan concept of god and temple. The Israelite God was not a local god, nor could He be localized. He was the transcendent One, whose being could not be limited to any physical structure and who needed no place of shelter or sanctuary.
>
> Furthermore, the Israelite God had no need for human provision. He was the One who provided for human need from an endless store of divine supply.... God's Presence did not dwell in the Israelite Temple in the same way a god was present in all the other pagan temples of the world. For this reason the God of Israel was not to be represented in form by an idol (Exodus 20:4; Deuteronomy 4:15-19) and placed in a shrine (Ezekiel 8:2-12) after the practice of the Canaanite religion.
>
> The Israelite Temple, rather than being a place where *God's needs* were met, was a place where God met the *needs of His people.*[5]

Ever since the Garden of Eden, it has been God's desire to fellowship with and establish a presence among His people. The Hebrew grammar in Genesis 3:8 suggests that the pre-fall Garden of Eden was a sanctuary where God met Adam and Eve for fellowship. "And they heard the sound of the LORD God walking in the garden in the cool of the day, and the man and his wife hid themselves from the presence of the LORD God among the trees of the garden."

After the intrusion of sin into the world, a holy God could no longer meet face-to-face with sinful humanity. Thus, expulsion from the sanctuary and the placing of angelic guards were necessary (Genesis 3:22-24).

In order for God to reestablish a holy presence and relationship with humanity in a sinful world, a sacred place must be established. Israel's Tabernacle, and later the Temple, met this need.

While God's general purpose was to establish His presence and show favor to His Chosen People, many other reasons are also apparent: the Temple was a daily reminder that God was a holy God and Israel a chosen nation; the priesthood and daily rituals demonstrated that in order for sinful people to come into God's presence, there must be an acceptable means of approach; the work foreshadowed in the daily sacrifices was that of Christ upon the cross; and it also taught that Israel must live a separate and holy life each and every day.

The Temple provides a physical and visible location for the holiness of heaven to dwell in the midst of fallen creation.

4. Where does the Bible teach about the Last Days' Temple?

The Bible speaks of two Temples in Israel's future. The first two Temples have come and gone, while the final two have yet to appear. The Tribulation Temple (the third Temple) will be next, while the Millennial Temple (the fourth Temple) will appear after Jesus the Messiah returns to planet Earth and builds it to use during His messianic kingdom.

The Tribulation Temple

There are no Bible verses that say, "There is going to be a third Temple." But the fact that there will be a Jewish Temple in Jerusalem at least by the midpoint of the seven-year tribulation period is supported by at least four scriptural references:

Daniel 9:27

> And he [Antichrist] will make a firm covenant with the many [the nation of Israel] for one week [seven years], but in the middle of the week [three-and-a-half years] he [Antichrist] will put a stop to sacrifice and grain offering; and on the wing of abominations [the altar in the Temple] will come one [Antichrist] who makes desolate, even until a complete destruction, one that is decreed, is poured out on the one [Antichrist] who makes desolate.

This passage predicts a future time-period of 7 years, during which the Antichrist defiles Israel's Temple by an evil act at the 3½ year point. In order for this to happen, there must be a Temple in Jerusalem. Therefore, we can conclude from this future event that the third Temple must be built and functioning by this time.

In the same way, Daniel 11:31 speaks of a future event, when "the regular sacrifice" will be abolished and *"the abomination of desolation"* will be set up in the third Temple. Prophecy scholar John Walvoord notes that the "temple of that future day will be desecrated much as Antiochus desecrated the temple in his day in the second century B.C., stopping the sacrifices and putting the temple to pagan use."[6] Daniel 12:11 also relates to this: "From the time that the regular sacrifice is abolished, and the abomination of desolation is set up, there will be 1,290 days."

Matthew 24:15,16

> Therefore when you see the ABOMINATION OF DESOLATION which was spoken of through Daniel the prophet, standing in the holy place (let the reader understand), then let those who are in Judea flee to the mountains.

When Jesus speaks of "the abomination of desolation... standing in the holy place," he is referring to the same event Daniel refers to in Daniel 9:27. The "holy place" is a reference to the most sacred room within Israel's Temple. What Temple? The third temple, since it is a future event. Dr. Tim LaHaye tells us that "Matthew 24:15 portrays the 'abomination of desolation,' when the Antichrist desecrates the rebuilt temple in Jerusalem." He then adds, "Obviously it has to be rebuilt in order to be desecrated."[7]

2 Thessalonians 2:3,4

> Let no one in any way deceive you, for it [the day of the Lord] will not come unless the apostasy comes first, and the man of lawlessness is revealed, the son of destruction [Antichrist], who opposes and exalts himself above every so called god or object of worship, so that he takes his seat in the temple of God, displaying himself as being God.

In this passage we see, for the third time, a description of "the abomination of desolation." This time it is referred to as the event in which Antichrist "takes his seat in the temple of God." Once again, which Temple? The clear answer is the future third Temple. Dr. Charles Ryrie tells us that at "the midpoint of the tribulation period the Antichrist will desecrate the rebuilt Jewish temple in Jerusalem by placing himself there to be worshiped."[8] This act of self-deification is the abomination of desolation.

Revelation 11:1,2

> And there was given me a measuring rod like a staff; and someone said, "Rise and measure the temple of God, and the altar, and those who worship in it. And leave out the court which is outside the temple, and do not measure it, for it has been given to the nations; and they will tread under foot the holy city for forty-two months."

Since the section of Revelation in which this passage appears takes place during the tribulation period, this is a reference to Israel's third Temple in Jerusalem.

The Millennial Temple

The Bible teaches in Ezekiel 40—48 that there will be a fourth Temple. This final Temple will be the center from which worship of Jesus Christ during the millennium will be focused.

> And He said to me, "Son of man, this is the place of My throne and the place of the soles of My feet, where I will dwell among the sons of Israel forever. And the house of Israel will not again defile My holy name, neither they nor their kings, by their harlotry and by the corpses of their kings when they die" (Ezekiel 43:7).

> As for you, son of man, describe the temple to the house of Israel, that they may be ashamed of their iniquities; and let them measure the plan (Ezekiel 43:10).

The Old Testament also refers to the sacrifices that will take place in the Millennial Temple in the following passages: Isaiah 56:7; 60:7,13; 66:20-23; Jeremiah 33:15-22; Zechariah 14:16-21.

P A R T   2

What Does the Bible Teach About Israel's Temples?

5. What does the Bible teach about the First Temple?

The First Temple (also known as Solomon's Temple) was constructed by the son of David, King Solomon, following the death of David. Although it had been David's desire to build the Temple, God did not permit this since David was a man of war rather than peace (see 1 Kings 5:3; 2 Samuel 7:1-13). Its purpose was to provide a permanent home for the ark of the covenant and the worship of the Lord.

Solomon began construction in the fourth year of his reign (ca. 967–960 B.C.) and completed it seven years later (1 Kings 6:1,37,38). The Bible gives detailed accounts of the Temple's construction in 1 Kings 5–8 and 2 Chronicles 2.

Solomon's Temple, following the dimensions of the Tabernacle, was about 3500 square feet, built on a 10 foot-high platform with 10 steps leading to the entrance. Two brass pillars, about 40 feet high and 12 feet in circumference, stood on each side of the entrance to the Temple. The first and smallest room of the Temple was a porch leading into the main room, the second of three rooms, referred to in the Bible as the Holy Place.

> The Holy Place's interior walls are covered with elaborately-carved cedar panels overlaid or inlaid with gold. The floors are covered with boards of cypress so that no stonework is seen. In addition to this, Solomon has adorned this room with beautiful precious stones.
>
> Housed within this awe-inspiring central chamber are the magnificent seven-branched *menorah* or candelabra, the table of showbread, bearing the sacred presence bread, and the Golden Altar of Incense, where aromatic spices are burned to mask the awful stench of the outside sacrifice. Also in this room were ten tables (five on the north side and five on the south), accompanied by ten lamps on lampstands, as well as numerous implements used in the priestly service.[9]

The Holy of Holies, the third and final room, was the most significant.

> Going on, we would be stopped from entrance into the *Devir*, the innermost room, by a double screen of a fabric veil and a wall whose only door is kept closed except on rare occasions. Access to this room, called "the Holy of Holies," is forbidden to all except the High Priest, and to him only once a year at *Yom Kippur*, the high holy Day of Atonement. In this room, a perfect cube about 35 feet each way, covered with 23 tons of gold, stands the great Ark of the Covenant, likewise covered in gold.

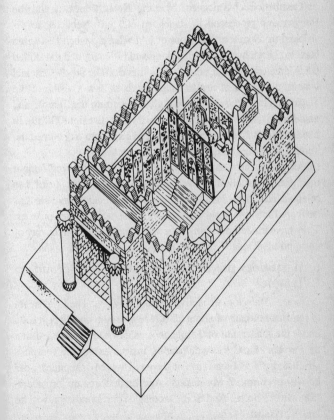

Solomon's Majestic Temple

The Ark rested on a bedrock platform called the *Even Shetiyyah* ("Foundation Stone").[10] The high priest rests the firepan on this rock when he enters the Holy of Holies.[11] (Later Jewish sources posit that this large rock mass was the foundation for the entire Temple, and that it merely broke through the ground at the point of the Holy of Holies.)[12]

As spiritual decline and idolatry dominated Israel year after year, God's judgment came upon the Northern Kingdom first, in 721 B.C. The Southern Kingdom, which included Judah and the Temple in Jerusalem became ripe for judgment 135 years later. The Lord, through His prophets, declared, "I will remove Judah also from My sight, as I have removed Israel. And I will cast off Jerusalem . . . and the temple" (2 Kings 23:27).

Destruction of Jerusalem by King Nebuchadnezzar and the Babylonians proceeded in stages. In 605 B.C. Nebuchadnezzar stripped the Southern Kingdom of its leadership when he carried back to Babylon as slaves their king and his court, and the skilled labor force (including Daniel and his friends). The prophet Ezekiel warned the nation of further judgment as he saw a vision of the *Shekinah* glory (the Presence of God) departing the Temple and vanishing over the Mount of Olives to the east (Ezekiel 10:18,19). In 586 B.C. the Babylonian army destroyed Jerusalem and burned the Temple (2 Kings 25:8,9; 2 Chronicles 36:18,19).

Jeremiah, the weeping prophet, gives the following lament over the destruction of Solomon's Temple: "The Lord has rejected His altar, He has abandoned His sanctuary; He has delivered into the hand of the enemy the walls of her palaces. They have made a noise in the house of the LORD as in the day of an appointed feast" (Lamentations 2:7).

6. What does the Bible teach about the Second Temple?

Israel's Babylonian captivity lasted 70 years. The Lord begin to return a remnant of about 50,000 Jews to the land in 538 B.C., under the leadership of Zerubbabel. Isaiah had prophesied that the Persian king Cyrus would be the instrument for the Temple's rebuilding: "It is I who says of Cyrus, 'He is My shepherd! And he will perform all My desire.' And he declares of Jerusalem, 'She will be built,' And of the temple, 'Your foundation will be laid.'" (Isaiah 44:28).

The book of Ezra in the Old Testament tells of Israel's efforts to rebuild the Temple. We find that, upon return to Jerusalem, the foundation for the Second Temple was laid, copying the Solomonic outline (Ezra 3:7-10). The Temple vessels and utensils were returned from Babylon, an altar constructed, sacrifices begun, and the observance of the biblical festivals restored (Ezra 1:7-11; 3:1-5). For the Jews, the restoration of the sacrificial system to the Temple constitutes a functioning Temple, regardless of how far along the rest of the construction has progressed.

Further construction of the Temple was halted due to the opposition from Samaritan residents of the Northern Kingdom, and was not resumed for another 15 years. The work was finally completed in 515 B.C., after a decree from the Persian king Darius who not only permitted the rebuilding, but prescribed local taxes (including those of the Samaritans!) to finance the construction (Ezra 6:1-15).

The Second Temple was a modest edifice when compared with Solomon's Temple. However, it was greatly enlarged and remodeled under Herod the Great, beginning in 20 B.C. Herod doubled the height of the original Second Temple and made it significantly wider. It is believed that Herod's improvements enabled the Second Temple to exceed in beauty and greatness Solomon's Temple—many thought it was the most beautiful building in the world. The Second Temple was regarded as one of the marvels of the ancient world. The historian Josephus tells us that the Temple was made of marble overlaid with gold, and appeared from a distance as a mountain of snow glistening in the sun. One of the sages of that time wrote, "He who has not seen Herod's building has not seen a beautiful building in his life."[13]

It is significant that our Lord Jesus Christ carried on His ministry during the Second Temple era. Many of the Gospel narratives and events in the book of Acts took place in Herod's Temple complex. The Jewish rejection of the Messiahship of Jesus revolves around that Temple. Christ, sitting on the Mount of Olives and looking at the Temple, wept over Jerusalem because of her rejection of Him and her impending judgment:

> O Jerusalem, Jerusalem, who kills the prophets and stones those who are sent to her! How often I wanted to gather your children together, the way a hen gathers her chicks under her wings, and you were unwilling. Behold, your house is being left to you desolate! For I say to you, from now on you shall not see Me until you say, "BLESSED IS HE WHO COMES IN THE NAME OF THE LORD!" (Matthew 23:37-39).

Judgment upon the nation Jerusalem, and the Temple began with an insurrection against Rome by Jewish zealots in A.D. 66.

A sensational act of defiance took place in the Temple when Eleazar, son of the captain of the Temple, ordered an end to the imperial sacrifice (which had been offered to the Emperor alongside the traditional Jewish service during the period of Roman rule). Rome's formidable Tenth Legion attempted to retake the Temple Mount, but failed, losing much equipment to the Jewish defenders.

The defiance, which became a full-scale revolt, soon secured all Judea in Jewish hands. Enraged by the success of this revolt, Emperor Nero sent Rome's best commander, Vespasian, with Rome's finest legions to crush the rebellion at all costs. By A.D. 69, after years of bitter fighting, the Romans had retaken all areas but Jerusalem, and Vespasian, who had recently succeeded Nero as Emperor, put his son, Titus, in charge of the Jerusalem campaign.

Following a siege of Jerusalem, Titus took counsel with the officers of his army concerning the fate of the Temple. There are conflicting reports as to the orders given. The Roman historian Tacitus records that the majority of the officers were in agreement that nothing less than the total destruction of the Temple would secure a lasting peace. Therefore, on the ninth day of the Jewish month of Av in A.D. 70, the city and the Temple were burned as Daniel had prophesied.

Josephus says that Titus had given specific orders that the Temple be left intact, and that a soldier acting on impulse, threw a torch through an archway of the Temple, setting the tapestries inside on fire. When the building burned, it is said that the gold on the walls melted and ran into the seams between the stones. Afterward, in an attempt to recover the gold, the Roman soldiers tore apart the stone walls, fulfilling precisely the prediction of Jesus that not one stone of the Temple would be left on another.[14]

Thus, the Second Temple came to the same end as had the First Temple. The destruction of the Temple in A.D. 70 has become the focus of forward-looking Jews who long for the construction and dedication of a Third Temple.

7. What does the Bible teach about the church as a spiritual Temple?

The New Testament teaches that the church—the body of Christ—is currently God's spiritual Temple. Just as God's presence was in the Garden of Eden, the Tabernacle, and Israel's Temple, so our Lord is currently present among His people today. The church is not a building, but consists of all those who have entered into a right relationship with God through the forgiveness of their sins by Christ's work on the cross.

The apostle Paul teaches that God's Spirit indwells all believers individually, and the church cooperately.

> Do you not know that you are a temple of God, and that the Spirit of God dwells in you? If any man destroys the temple of God, God will destroy him, for the temple of God is holy, and that is what you are (1 Corinthians 3:16,17).

> You are no longer strangers and aliens, but you are fellow citizens with the saints, and are of God's household, having been built upon the foundation of the apostles and prophets, Christ Jesus Himself being the corner stone, in whom the whole building, being fitted together is growing into a holy temple in the Lord; in whom you also are being built together into a dwelling of God in the Spirit (Ephesians 2:19-22).

Today God's presence is not located in a stone temple, but in a Temple of living stones—the individual believers in Christ. Knowing a believer's current relationship with God through Christ should lead to pure and godly living, since a Temple is supposed to be representative of God and His standards.

The fact that the church is a spiritual Temple today does not conflict with the notion that God's plan includes two more stone Temples in the future, any more than the fact that because a Tabernacle once existed, that precluded a future Temple in Jerusalem. Belief that the church is a spiritual Temple and that God still has two more stone Temples in His plan for history are not mutually exclusive viewpoints.

8. What does the Bible teach about the Third Temple?

We noted in Question 4 the scriptural support for the future Third Temple. This Temple is also called Antichrist's Temple because he will defile it by setting up his image in the Holy of Holies. This blasphemous act is known in the Bible as "the abomination of desolation" (Daniel 9:27; 11:31; 12:11; Matthew 24:15; Mark 13:14; 2 Thessalonians 2:4; Revelation 13:15). It is also referred to as the Tribulation Temple, because it will come into existence at least by the midpoint of that seven-year period (Daniel 9:27).

This Temple will play a central role in end-time events relating to Israel's national restoration during her final seven years of history (Daniel 9:24-27), which prepares her for acceptance of Jesus as Messiah just prior to the Second Advent.

The book of Revelation carries on an interesting interplay between the Antichrist's Temple on earth during the tribulation (Revelation 11:1,2) and "the temple of God which is in heaven" (Revelation 11:19). A military dictum is "take the high ground." Our Sovereign God's position in heaven certainly follows such a strategy, as He originates His judgment upon the Christ-rejecting earth-dwellers below, who are hunkered down within the rocks and caves.

The Tribulation Temple is mentioned in Revelation 11:1-2:

> And there was given me a measuring rod like a staff; and someone said, "Rise and measure the temple of God, and the altar, and those who worship in it. And leave out the court which is outside the temple, and do not measure it, for it has been given to the nations; and they will tread under foot the holy city for forty-two months."

Why does God command John to measure this Temple? Old Testament passages, such as Ezekiel 40 and Zechariah 2, link measurement with a spiritual evaluation of the people. Hal Lindsey notes,

> [God's] appraisal of this future Temple therefore determines whether it's truly fulfilling its intended purpose. Unfortunately, it turns out to be an apostate place of worship. Its reconstruction is not based on a recognition

DANIEL'S SEVENTY WEEKS
(490 Years)

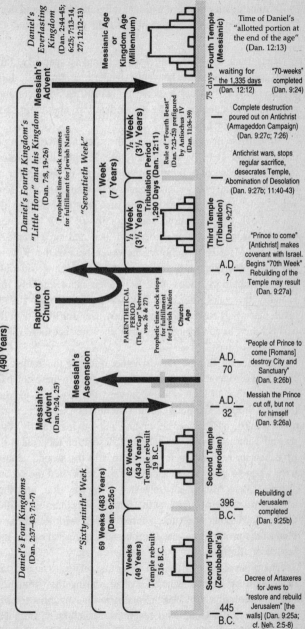

Daniel's Four Kingdoms (Dan. 2:37–43; 7:1–7)

Daniel's Everlasting Kingdom (Dan. 2:44–45; 6:25; 7:13–14, 27; 12:12–13)

Messianic Age or Kingdom Age (Millennium)

Messiah's Advent

Daniel's Fourth Kingdom's "Little Horn" and his Kingdom
(Dan. 7:8, 19–26)

Prophetic time clock resumes for fulfillment for Jewish Nation

"Seventieth Week"

Time of Daniel's "allotted portion at the end of the age" (Dan. 12:13)

Fourth Temple (Messianic)

75 days — waiting for the 1,335 days (Dan. 12:12)

"70-weeks" completed (Dan. 9:24)

1 Week (7 Years)

½ Week (3½ Years) — ½ Week (3½ Years)

Tribulation Period (Dan. 12:11)

1,290 Days (Dan. 12:11)

Rule of "Fourth Beast" (Dan. 7:23–25) prefigured by Antiochus IV (Dan. 11:36–39)

Complete destruction poured out on Antichrist (Armageddon Campaign) (Dan. 9:27c; 7:26)

Antichrist wars, stops regular sacrifice, desecrates Temple, Abomination of Desolation (Dan. 9:27b; 11:40–43)

Third Temple (Tribulation) (Dan. 9:27)

A.D. ? — "Prince to come" [Antichrist] makes covenant with Israel. Begins "70th Week" Rebuilding of the Temple may result (Dan. 9:27a)

Rapture of Church

PARENTHETICAL PERIOD (The "Gap" between vss. 26 & 27) Prophetic time clock stops for fulfillment for Jewish Nation

Church Age

Messiah's Advent (Dan. 9:24, 25)

Messiah's Ascension

A.D. 70 — "People of Prince to come [Romans] destroy City and Sanctuary" (Dan. 9:26b)

A.D. 32 — Messiah the Prince cut off, but not for himself (Dan. 9:26a)

"Sixty-ninth" Week

62 Weeks (434 Years) Temple rebuilt 19 B.C.

69 Weeks (483 Years) (Dan. 9:25c)

Second Temple (Herodian)

396 B.C. — Rebuilding of Jerusalem completed (Dan. 9:25b)

7 Weeks (49 Years) Temple rebuilt 516 B.C.

Second Temple (Zerubbabel's)

445 B.C. — Decree of Artaxeres for Jews to "restore and rebuild Jerusalem" [the walls] (Dan. 9:25a; cf. Neh. 2:5-8)

of Jesus as the Messiah, but on a nationalistic desire to once again possess a national religious symbol and draw the people back to a belief in their God.[15]

Measurement of the Antichrist's Temple, especially, fails when compared with the heavenly standard mentioned by John in Revelation 11:19. Such a shortcoming justifies God's continuation of judgment upon the earth-dwellers and their false Temple and worship.

Some Bible interpreters say that the reference to the Temple in Revelation 11:1,2 is not to a future Temple, that it refers instead to the second Temple, or is a figure of speech for an apostate spiritual entity such as Israel or the church. But, if these verses refer to the second Temple of Christ's time, then the whole book of Revelation, and virtually all New Testament prophecy would have already been fulfilled, and some people do teach this. Most Bible scholars, however, believe that Revelation was not written until well after A.D. 70, which would make this interpretation impossible. It is even more unlikely that virtually the whole book of Revelation would have already taken place.[16] If Revelation has already been fulfilled, then the early church lived through this time unaware that these things had come to pass.

The spiritual Temple view, whether referring to Israel or the church, is erroneous because the use of *temple* in these contexts is not intended to be taken figuratively. For example, in Matthew 24, Jesus is speaking about a literal Temple, since, in the context of the passage, he is standing and looking directly at the second Temple. The abomination of desolation took place the first time through Antiochus Epiphanes in the second century B.C., when he stopped the sacrifices and desecrated the second Temple by sacrificing an unclean pig on the altar, and then setting up a statue of Jupiter at the Temple. This literally fulfilled Daniel 11:31. Therefore, these future events will be similar in kind to the prototypes—they will be real, historical events in a last days' Temple.

The biblical role for the Third Temple relates to an apostate restoration of Israel's worship system during the tribulation. Such a restoration provides the platform for Antichrist to challenge and insult God, who responds in judgment from His heavenly Temple. Thus, the Third Temple will play a central role in end-time events within the program of God.

9. What does the Bible teach about the Fourth Temple?

· Destined to be perhaps the most beautiful and magnificent building in human history, the Fourth Temple (or Millennial Temple) is discussed in detail in Ezekiel 40:5–43:27. This will be Israel's final Temple in history and will exist during the 1000 year reign of Jesus the Messiah from Jerusalem. The Millennial Temple will be the focus of all the world. Israel and her Temple will serve as the center for the priestly rituals and offerings that will provide guidance in the worship of Jesus the Messiah.

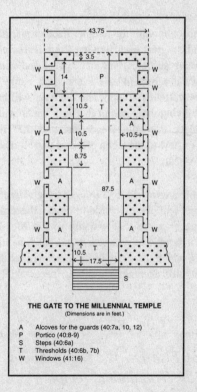

THE GATE TO THE MILLENNIAL TEMPLE
(Dimensions are in feet.)

A   Alcoves for the guards (40:7a, 10, 12)
P   Portico (40:8-9)
S   Steps (40:6a)
T   Thresholds (40:6b, 7b)
W   Windows (41:16)

Dr. John Walvoord describes the Millennial Temple and its worship:

The temple to be built in the Millennium will be much larger than any historic temple of Israel, being a square 875 feet (500 cubits) in width and length. Like previous temples, it will face east and will have an outer wall on the other three sides. The temple will have thirty rooms built on three levels. Except for the western wall, the other three sides will have a large outer court that will surround the temple itself with gates in each of the three walls....

Various regulations were issued by Ezekiel concerning the functions of the priests and Levites in the temple worship. Special sacrifices were to be offered on the first month and the first day (46:18-19). The Passover feast is also mentioned as being observed on the first month of the fourteenth day, an event that followed the seven-day feast of unleavened bread (45:21-25).

...In connection with the temple, Ezekiel predicted that there will be a great river flowing from the temple to the south, having sufficient volume so that one will not be able to wade across (47:3-6). The river banks will be covered with trees (vv. 7-9), and the river will have fish and other living creatures in it. Fresh water will apparently replace the salty Dead Sea, and the river will continue to flow to the south of Israel until it reaches the Gulf of Arabah.[17]

Since the millennium will be a time in which Israel will be exalted and Christ will rule the world through a theocracy from Jerusalem, it makes sense that worship of the Messiah will revolve around a Temple. It will be a wondrous time indeed; it will be a time in which the glory of the Lord will return to the Temple as Israel fulfills her national calling (see Ezekiel 43:1-5).

P A R T   3

What Else Do We Know About the Tribulation Temple?

10. Have there been attempts to build the Third Temple in modern times?

The Jews have attempted to rebuild the Temple a number of times since the destruction of the Second Temple in A.D. 70. On a few occasions, they have met with limited and temporary success but nothing approaching the building of the first two Temples.

After the destruction of the Temple in A.D. 70, life in Jerusalem for the remaining Jews tumbled into deep decline because of the absence of their center of life—the Temple. The empty Temple Mount became the focus of their hopes and dreams. These hopes were ignited when the Roman emperor Publius Aelius Hadrian began his reign in A.D. 117. Apparently, official contacts were made between Judean Jews and the Roman government under Hadrian, and permission was granted to begin rebuilding the Temple.

Jewish hopes for a revival ended in A.D. 129, when Hadrian came to Jerusalem to begin erection of a Roman colony on the ruins of the city. In A.D. 132, a revolt erupted under the Jewish leader Shimon bar Kosiba (who was renamed *Bar Kochba* "Son of the Star," by Talmudic Sage Rabbi Akiva, who heralded him as the messiah).

The Revolt repulsed the Roman garrisons, and the Jewish rebels managed to hold Jerusalem for almost three years. During this time, an independent government was established and Bar Kokhba proclaimed himself the messiah. He began rebuilding the Temple and resumed the Temple ritual, perhaps including the reinstitution of sacrifice.[18]

The principal evidence for a Bar Kokhba Temple stems from coins that he minted bearing a picture of the facade of the Temple and the name of Eleazer, his high priest.[19]

Bar Kokhba's reign ended when Hadrian recaptured Jerusalem in A.D. 135. The emperor destroyed the Bar Kokhba Temple,[20] and erected a temple to the Roman trio of Juno, Jupiter, and Minerva, along with an equestrian statue of himself on the Temple Mount.

In the following centuries, several attempts were made to organize a Temple rebuilding effort. The most significant of these occurred during the 19 month reign of Flavius Claudius Julianus, known in history as "Julian the Apostate," because of his defection from Christianity. Julian attempted to rebuild the Temple in Jerusalem in the hopes that this would discredit Christianity.

In A.D. 363, Julian arranged for funds and building materials to be provided, and appointed Alypius of Antioch to oversee the reconstruction. Christian sources tell of multitudes of Jews returning to Jerusalem to assist in the project. Then the unexpected happened. Just as the builders were attempting to break into the foundations on the Temple Mount, an earthquake—not uncommon to the region—interrupted the attempt. The earthquake apparently ignited reservoirs of trapped gases below ground, and the resulting explosion destroyed the building materials on the site. Julian died shortly after that—and with it went Jewish hopes.

Other failed attempts occurred under Empress Eudocia in A.D. 443, and under Persian rule in A.D. 614–17.[21] Attempts to rebuild the Jewish Temple in Jerusalem, since these early efforts, have resumed only in the last few decades. However, all of these attempts did strengthen Jewish resolve and focus their attention upon a future rebuilt Temple. During the intervening years of persecution endured throughout the Diaspora, it is not surprising that their motto became, "Next Year in Jerusalem."

11. Who owns and controls the Temple Mount today?

As a result of Jewish victory and conquest during the Six Day War in June 1967, the Temple Mount was briefly under complete Israeli control—on the third day of the war, Israeli troops gained control of the Temple Mount. However, after the war, on June 17, 1967, Defense Minister Moshe Dayan met with members of the Supreme Moslem Council (known also as the Waqf or Wakf) which oversaw Islamic holy sites. The meeting was set to determine how the Temple Mount would be administered. By the end of the negotiations, control of the Temple Mount was returned to Moslem hands after only ten days of Israeli jurisdiction. A recounting of the meeting and outcome is sobering; the results were incredible and, to many, incomprehensible:

> Dayan had already ordered the Israeli flag removed from on top of the Dome of the Rock on the afternoon of the Old City's liberation. The discussion with the Moslems led to further concessions. The administrative control over the Temple Mount was to be the sole responsibility of the Supreme Moslem Council—the Waqf. Though the Jews would be permitted free access to the Mount, prayer or public worship by Jews was prohibited.... The Israeli government then allocated responsibility of the Temple Mount area to different groups.... The top of the Temple Mount, however, the site of the First and Second Temple, was given to the Moslems to administrate. Though they

allow tourists to visit they do not allow freedom of worship or any non-Moslem archeological activity.[22]

The concessions of Dayan caught religious Jews totally off-guard. They never imagined that such a thing would happen. Why did Dayan do it? Dayan, a secular Jew, had worked for many years with Arabs as an officer in the British military. Since the religious aspects of the modern state of Israel were overshadowed by his political concerns, he saw the Temple Mount as a bargaining chip which he hoped would appease the Moslems and make them easier to govern under Israeli presence. He said of the Temple Mount, "I have no doubt that because the power is in our hands we must take a stand based on yielding. We must view the Temple Mount as a historic site relating to past memory."[23]

Dayan's actions became a hindrance, rather than a help. The religious Jews were angered and the Moslems were not appeased. This act has been at the center of much of the contemporary Arab-Israeli conflict. Control of the Temple Mount became fertile ground for the establishment of many Jewish organizations seeking the building of the Third Temple. The division of the Temple Mount area remains today as it was in 1967—the Temple Mount proper is under the administration of the Waqf. Altercations continue to erupt and gain national and international media coverage over the prohibition of Jewish worship on the Mount (though not all Jewish religious leaders and followers believe it necessary or even desirable).[24]

Ownership and control of the Temple Mount are two different things. The state of Israel owns the Temple Mount; the Moslem Waqf controls it. The current situation with the Temple Mount is somewhat similar to a developer who owns a tract of land and desires to build on it. However, he cannot do so without the approval of other authorities. In the case of the Temple, the building permit (approval and acquiescence) will indeed take a miracle. Ultimately providence, not politics, will prevail.

12. What are the plans and preparations for Israel's next Temple?

Many plans are being made for a rebuilt Temple,[25] and many diverse groups in Israel are preparing for it. Some of the organizations and activities include:

The Temple Mount Faithful, led by Gershon Salomon, who use activist measures in an attempt to motivate fellow countrymen to rebuild the Temple. One act has been their periodic attempt to lay a four-and-a-half ton cornerstone upon the Temple Mount. Activist Gershon Salomon demonstrates his resolve when he says,

> In the right day—I believe it is very soon—this stone will be put on the Temple Mount, and be worked and polished ... and will be the first stone for the Third Temple. Just now this stone lays not far from the Temple Mount, very close to the Walls of the Old City of Jerusalem, near Shechem Gate ... and this stone watches over the Temple Mount. But the day is not far that this stone will be in the right place—it can be today ... or tomorrow, we are very close to the right time."[26]

Another act they've instituted has been the sacrifice of animals.

The Temple Institute, headed by Israel Ariel, has made almost all of the 102 utensils needed for Temple worship according to biblical and rabbinic standards. These are on display for tourists to see at the Temple Institute tourist center in the Old City in Jerusalem.

The Ateret Cohanim has established a yeshiva (religious school) for the education and training of Temple priests. Their task is to research regulations, gather qualified Levites, and train them for a future priesthood.

Many yeshivas have arisen throughout Jerusalem to prepare for the eventuality of a rebuilt, fully functioning Temple service. Clothing is being made, harps constructed, computer-designed architectural plans made, and some rabbis are deciding what modern innovations can be adopted into a new Temple. Also, an effort is well underway to secure kosher animals for sacrifice, including red heifers. And some people continue to seek daily prayer upon the Temple Mount to help prepare the way.

Many other preparations are currently underway for Israel's return to all aspects of Temple worship.

13. What prevents Jewish construction of the Temple today?

There are significant political and theological obstacles to the rebuilding of the Temple. From a Jewish theological perspective, there is no agreement on when or even if the Temple should be rebuilt by human hands. Although some Jewish groups are making preparations for the rebuilding, other groups and segments within Judaism do not favor these preparations:

> Even among the ultra-Orthodox themselves there are several interpretations concerning how the Temple can be rebuilt. The Jewish sages, speaking from the distant perspective of the Diaspora, taught that the Temple must await the coming of the Messiah. Maimonides also argued that only the Messiah could build the Temple.... The Israeli government agrees with this position and maintains that their actions to prohibit Jews from worshipping on the Temple Mount are based on these rather than political grounds.... Other groups, however, believe the Temple may be built at the present time by whatever means possible. Proponents of this position note that the Babylonian Talmud has conflicting opinions about the matter and that the Jerusalem Talmud permits the Jews to construct an intermediate edifice before the messianic era.[27]

Not only are there Jewish theological differences as noted above, there are also significant political and religious issues at stake with the Islamic world. The Waqf controls the Temple Mount and so long as that remains the same, no rebuilding will occur. The Dome of the Rock stands firmly on the Temple Mount, and the entire area is a Muslim sacred site. If the Temple is to be rebuilt on the Temple Mount, then only two logical possibilities exist for the Dome of the Rock and the Al Aqsa Mosque: These sacred structures must either be moved or destroyed. Either one of these options, in today's political climate, would cause a monumental war between Israel and the Arab world.

Although the technology exists to move and relocate these structures, there is no indication that this would ever be entertained as an option from a Muslim perspective. While it is conceivable that the structures could be destroyed as a result of war or terrorism, this also does not seem likely. Some Jews believe that natural disasters, such as a series of earthquakes, might also destroy the sites. Even so, it is unlikely that the Temple Mount would be abandoned by the Muslims. In fact, in the past when this has occurred, the Dome has been quickly repaired.

But should these Muslim sites be destroyed by a natural disaster or by a human agency, either accidentally or on purpose, there is every reason to suspect that the Muslims would simply rebuild them as they have done repeatedly in the past. The solution to the rebuilding of the Temple must rest on a greater event, one that dramatically affects the religious and political situation in Israel.[28]

Even in the unlikely event that something caused the 35 acres of the Temple Mount to be scraped clean of current structures, it would not solve the political problems associated with this holy site. Islam would still consider it their holy territory and would treat it as if their holy places remained.

Any current attempts to rebuild the Temple will likely meet with fierce political and religious opposition from many sides. Yet, in turbulent times, events can happen quickly. Although it might seem unlikely, it is not unthinkable that the rebuilding could start soon.

Many people who have followed the history of the Zionist Movement—which worked for a return to and establishment of the modern state of Israel—know that similar obstacles stood in the way of the establishment of the modern state of Israel. Yet the events of history lead to the impossible—the state of Israel. Perhaps, in a similar way, the Temple will be rebuilt.

14. When will Israel's Temple be rebuilt?

From a Christian perspective, there is nothing biblically or theologically that prohibits or teaches that the Temple cannot be rebuilt prior to the rapture or in our own day, even though all biblical references to the Tribulation Temple occur during the future seven-year period known as the tribulation. The Temple may be rebuilt prior to the rapture and tribulation—like the way Israel, in our own day, returned to the land before events of the tribulation have begun.

The fact that there are many movements and organizations in Israel today that are planning and preparing for the Third Temple only heightens our expectation that problems will soon be resolved and construction may soon begin.[29] The only biblical requirement is that the Temple has to be rebuilt and functioning by the mid-point of the seven-year tribulation.

One speculation about a possible scenario, based upon a model of future events derived from Scripture, unfolds as follows: There are differing views among scholars concerning when the battle of Gog and Magog will take place in relation to God's plan for the last days (see Ezekiel 38–39). It is most likely that this battle will occur during a relatively short time span just after the rapture, but before the start of the tribulation, which will gain a window of European sympathy for Israel. Israel's great losses, particularly under an Arab-Russian league, will be compensated with complete sovereignty over the Temple Mount and permission to rebuild the Third Temple. Likely, control of the Temple Mount for Israel will be part of a settlement gained in negotiations between Israel and the European leader (the antichrist), which, when signed, will start the seven-year tribulation period (Daniel 9:24-27).

This scenario solves the problem of moving the Arabs and their Dome of the Rock from the Mount, since Israel would receive full control of it as a result of a war. Israel's control of the Temple Mount would not start a war, since one will have just ended. Israel will also have gained permission from the West, which will be in control of the world through Antichrist, to rebuild. Since the Temple has to be built only by the mid-point of the seven-year period, Israel will have plenty of time, especially in light of modern technology and preparations now being made. This time the Jewish people will not delay or return the Temple Mount to the Arabs as Moshe Dayan did in 1967.

We believe that this speculation makes sense in light of the biblical framework; but, it is merely speculation in terms of known events.

15. Where on the Temple Mount will the next Temple be located?

All agree that the Third Temple will be built somewhere on the 35-acre Temple Mount in Jerusalem. But precisely where the relatively small Temple will be placed upon the Mount is a source of great debate. What are the options?

Three sites have received the most attention as possible Temple locations: the Northern site, the Traditional site, and the Southern site.

The Southern Site

The least likely is the Southern site, which was proposed by Catholic scholar Bellarmino Bagatti in 1979.[30] Bagatti concluded from his study of ancient documents and his personal

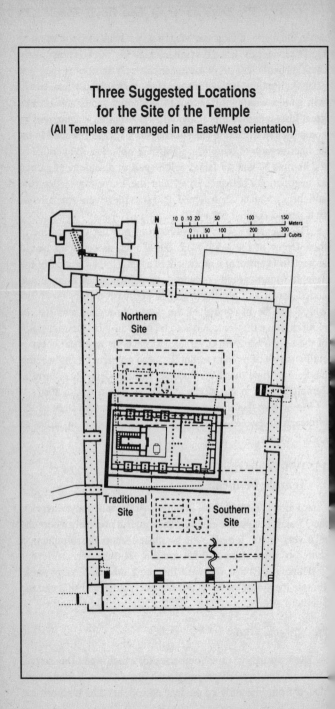

Three Suggested Locations
for the Site of the Temple
(All Temples are arranged in an East/West orientation)

exploration and measurements, that the ancient Temple must have occupied a site to the south, somewhere between the Dome of the Rock and the Al-Aqsa Mosque.

Bagatti's view is the weakest of the three views because it is based, at crucial points, upon false historical data that was used for his operating assumptions. One of his false assumptions is that the sacred rock at the top of the Temple Mount is not a basis for locating the Temple.

The Northern Site

Dr. Asher Kaufman of Israel, in the late 1970's, developed a view that the Temple was located at the northeastern corner of the Temple Mount, with an east-west line aligning the Mount of Olives with the Eastern Gate and the Temple exactly bisecting the small cupola at the place of the Holy of Holies. He believes that this point is the highest natural point on the Temple Mount, and where the Temple would be located.[31]

Israeli archaeologist Dr. Dan Bahat raises the following objections to Kaufman's view:

> We [archaeologists] do not accept the view of Dr. Asher Kaufman. His placement of the Temple does not agree in any way with what we know today about the arrangement of the Temple Mount. There is another Temple Mount that dates either from the Hasmonean period or of that of Simon the Just (we cannot precisely set the date as of yet), and it was a Temple Mount that was confined precisely to the topography of the area. It was made in such a way that *no* addition to it could have been made by anybody without disturbing the topographical features. For example, the central valley of Jerusalem starts at a point that goes down to where the Western Wall is today, and from this point goes under the Temple Mount in order to come outside down below.
>
> This is the reason why when Herod the Great wanted to enlarge the Temple Mount, because he could not build it without topographical disturbances, and because the Hasmoneans, or Simon the Just, had made the largest expansion of the Temple possible within the framework of the topography around the Temple Mount. Herod the

Great, therefore, in order to make his enlargement, had to overpass the central valley and other surrounding valleys in Jerusalem. Therefore we know *precisely* the conditions of how the Temple was installed prior to the time of Herod the Great.

If we take Asher Kaufman's theory of the location of the Holy of Holies, it will force the entire Temple to be built beyond the northern valley of the Temple Mount, and this is an *impossibility* because of the great depth of the valley below. Moreover, Charles Warren discovered an enormous moat in this northern area, and if we accept Kaufman's theory, half the Temple would have to be built within this moat.[32]

This view has gained popularity among some American Evangelicals as a solution that would overcome the political problems associated with rebuilding the Temple. Some have suggested that if the Northern view is correct, the Temple could be built without disturbing the Dome of the Rock. However, this is no solution, since neither religious Jews nor Arabs would allow the close presence of the other's edifice to defile their holy place.

The Traditional Site

The view held by most religious Jews in Israel today, is that the traditional site, as preserved by the Dome of the Rock, is where the next Temple will be built. This is the view we believe to be correct. Nevertheless, it really doesn't matter what anyone thinks—other than the Jews making the decisions when the time comes.

While many details could be given in support of this view, it comes down to a simple fact—the Dome of the Rock preserves the rock, and thus the spot of prior Temples. Dan Bahat says unequivocally:

I will say right now that the Temple is standing exactly where the Dome of the Rock is today on the Temple Mount. I want to say explicitly and clearly that we believe that the Rock under the Dome is the *precise site* of the Holy of Holies. The Temple extended *exactly* to the place where the Dome is. The "Foundation Stone" is actually that stone which comprised the Holy of Holies.[33]

Chaimi Richman of the Temple Institute says:

> We have a tradition that has been passed down in an unbroken chain from our fathers that the Rock, the stone underneath the Dome of the Rock, is the "foundation stone."[34]

Dan Bahat agrees with this when he adds:

> If this site were not the site of the Temple, we would not have the sanctity that has been bestowed upon that stone for centuries. The Church fathers describe how the Jews were coming every year to that place, and the Moslems chose to build their sanctuary on the very same stone because they were aware of the Jewish tradition.... Omar, the Moslem conqueror of Jerusalem was brought by a Jew straight to that stone and not to another one. So the tradition is quite clear about the tradition of this place.[35]

The Bible does not require that the Temple be built upon a specific site in Jerusalem in order to fulfill the prophecy. However, the Jewish point of view believes that it must be built where earlier Temples once stood. At this time, the overwhelming belief within Jewish circles is that it will be built where the current Dome of the Rock now stands. They believe that if the Temple could be built somewhere other than the Temple Mount, it would have been constructed long ago.

16. Does the Ark of the Covenant relate to the rebuilding of the Temple?

It is hard to make a clear case from the Bible that the Ark of the Covenant is related to the rebuilding of the Temple. While there are many Jewish traditions that the Ark of the Covenant and other Temple vessels must be found and restored to a rebuilt Temple, they are not directly supported by Scripture.[36] The Bible does not directly state that the ancient Ark of the Covenant will be restored to the Third Temple. Dr. Randall Price attempts to make a scriptural case that the ancient Ark of the Covenant will be recovered for the Third Temple:

This passage [2 Chronicles 36:18,19] reveals that the Temple and its vessels are inseparable; therefore the destiny of the two must be prophetically linked as well....

Just as the Temple was destroyed first by the Babylonians and later by the Romans (Jeremiah 7:14; Luke 21:5,6, 20-24), so, too, were the Temple vessels taken away (2 Kings 24:13; Jeremiah 27:16-22). Yet, just as the Temple was (and is) to be rebuilt (Daniel 9:16,17,20-27), so also will these treasures be restored. Support for this deduction may be found in Jeremiah 27:22.... Isaiah also predicted this restoration of the vessels [Isaiah 52:11-12].

Jeremiah and Isaiah were speaking about the first restoration of the Temple when the Jewish people returned from Babylon (Jeremiah 28:1-6), but their prophecies set a pattern for the predicted second return (Isaiah 11:11; Ezekiel 36:24-28) and restoration of the Temple.... Just as Jeremiah and Isaiah predicted the overthrow of Babylon and the restoration of Israel in the past, so also did John predict the same for the future (Revelation 17–20). If the first destruction of 587 B.C. was followed by reconstruction, why not the second destruction in A.D. 70 as well? And if the vessels were part of the Second Temple, should they not be a part of the Third? The Jeremiah text implies that the answer is yes.[37]

The basic problem with Dr. Price's presentation is that he is drawing deductions from assumptions. None of the passages cited establish a factual basis for his deductions.

The Ark of the Covenant may be found and restored to the Third Temple, but there is no biblical basis for making such a claim. Certainly, if an Ark of antiquity were found, perhaps under the Temple Mount, then it would provide a strong argument to many in Israel that the only suitable place to house it would be in a rebuilt Temple. It could further be argued that God's providence is with them, since His Hand has provided the most important piece of furniture in the Temple.

It could happen that the Ark will be found, but the Bible does not require it. Israel could fulfill her need for Temple artifacts by restocking a rebuilt Temple with newly crafted ones, including the Ark of the Covenant, if they decided that one should be placed into the Third Temple.

P A R T   4

What Else Do We Know About the Millennial Temple?

17. Why will there be a Millennial Temple?

The purpose of the Millennial Temple is found in Ezekiel 37:26-28:

> And I will make a covenant of peace with them; it will be an everlasting covenant with them. And I will place them and multiply them, and will set My sanctuary in their midst forever. My dwelling place also will be with them; and I will be their God, and they will be My people. And the nations will know that I am the Lord who sanctifies Israel, when My sanctuary is in their midst forever.

The Lord declares that the Millennial Temple will be one of the ways in which His name is known to the nations and in which He is vindicated. In Ezekiel 37:21-28, we are told that at the second coming of Christ several promises for Israel will be fulfilled. One of these promises is the presence of God in His new sanctuary, the Millennial Temple. Just as God dwelled in the Tabernacle with Israel upon their deliverance from Egypt, so also will He again "tabernacle" with His people upon their acceptance of Jesus Christ as Messiah.

18. Why will there be sacrifices in the Millennial Temple?

One aspect of the Millennial Temple described in Ezekiel 40–46, especially 43:13-27, which has given many prophecy students pause for reflection is the purpose and role of future sacrifices. At least four other Old Testament prophets join Ezekiel in affirming a sacrificial system in a Millennial Temple (see Isaiah 56:7; 66:20-23; Jeremiah 33:18; Zechariah 14:16-21; Malachi 3:3-4).

If we accept the literal interpretation of a millennial sacrificial system, are we contradicting passages such as Hebrews 7:26,27 and 9:26, which teach that Jesus Christ was the perfect and final sacrifice for sin? Premillennial scholars fully recognize the issues at hand here. Dr. John F. Walvoord has noted this concern and writes:

The only real problem in connection with a future literal temple is not the question as to whether such a temple could be built in the millennium, but the fact that this would indicate also a literal interpretation of the temple ritual and sacrifices.... The question is naturally raised why the sacrifices should be observed in the millennium if the sacrifice of Christ once and for all fulfilled the typical expectation of the Old Testament sacrificial system. While other objections are also made of a lesser character, it is obvious that this constitutes the major obstacle, not only to accepting the sacrificial system but the possibility of the future temple in the millennium as well.[38]

There are at least two legitimate solutions to this question. First, many students and teachers of prophecy have noted that the sacrifices may function as a memorial to the work of Christ. Dr. Jerry Hullinger summarized this view:

According to this view the sacrifices offered during the earthly reign of Christ will be visible reminders of His work on the cross. Thus, these sacrifices will not have any efficacy except to memorialize Christ's death. The primary support for this argument is the parallel of the Lord's Supper. It is argued that just as the communion table looks back on the Cross without besmirching its glory, so millennial sacrifices will do the same.[39]

This view does not, however, completely resolve all the concerns. Ezekiel says that the sacrifices are *for atonement* rather than a memorial (Ezekiel 45:15,17,20). Therefore, a second solution to the question of why is that the sacrifices are for ceremonial purification. Rather than merely a memorial view, Dr. Hullinger suggests:

...a solution that maintains dispensational distinctives, deals honestly with the text of Ezekiel, and in no way demeans the work Christ did on the cross. This study suggests that animal sacrifices during the millennium will serve primarily to remove ceremonial uncleanness and prevent defilement from polluting the temple envisioned by Ezekiel. This will be necessary because the glorious presence of Yahweh will once again be dwelling on earth in the midst of a sinful and unclean people.[40]

Dr. Hullinger concludes by saying:

> Because of God's promise to dwell on earth during the millennium (as stated in the New Covenant), it is necessary that He protect His presence through sacrifice.... It should further be added that this sacrificial system will be a temporary one in that the millennium (with its partial population of unglorified humanity) will last only one thousand years. During the eternal state all inhabitants of the New Jerusalem will be glorified and will therefore not be a source of contagious impurities to defile the holiness of Yahweh.[41]

The presence and purpose of sacrifices as understood above neither diminishes the work of Christ, nor violates the normal and literal interpretation of the prophetic passages. Although there will be sacrifices, the focus of all worship will remain on the person and work of the Savior.

The sacrifices of the Millennial Temple will not be a return to the Mosaic Law, since the Law has forever been fulfilled and discontinued through Christ (see Romans 6:14,15; 7:1-6; 1 Corinthians 9:20,21; 2 Corinthians 3:7-11; Galatians 4:1-7; 5:18; Hebbrews 8:13; 10:1-14). Instead, as Dr. Arnold Fruchtenbaum notes:

> ...there will be a sacrificial system instituted in the Millennium that will have some features similar to the Mosaic system, along with some new laws. For that very reason, the sacrificial system of the Millennium must not be viewed as a reinstitution of the Mosaic system because it is not. It will be a new system that will contain some things old and some things new and will be instituted for an entirely different purpose.[42]

19. What is the origin of the Millennial Temple?

The Bible indicates that Jesus, the Messiah of Israel, who is known prophetically as the "Branch" will personally build the Millennial Temple.

> And take silver and gold, make an ornate crown, and set it
> on the head of Joshua the son of Jehozadak, the high
> priest. Then say to him, "Thus says the LORD of hosts,
> 'Behold, a man whose name is Branch, for He will branch
> out from where He is; and He will build the temple of the
> LORD. Yes, it is He who will build the temple of the LORD,
> and He who will bear the honor and sit and rule on His
> throne. Thus, He will be a priest on His throne, and the
> counsel of peace will be between the two offices.' "
> (Zechariah 6:11-13).

Perhaps He will bring the Temple with Him from heaven at
some point during Second Coming events.

At the second advent, important topographical changes will
occur to the land of Israel in order to facilitate the huge Millennial Temple.

> And in that day His feet will stand on the Mount of Olives,
> which is in front of Jerusalem on the east; and the Mount
> of Olives will be split in its middle from east to west by a
> very large valley, so that half of the mountain will move
> toward the north and the other half toward the south
> (Zechariah 14:4).

In conjunction with a new platform to accommodate the
Millennial Temple, Jerusalem and the land around the City of
David will be elevated in preparation for Israel's key role during
Messiah's rule:

> And the LORD will be king over all the earth; in that day
> the LORD will be the only one, and His name the only one.
> All the land will be changed into a plain from Geba to
> Rimmon south of Jerusalem; but Jerusalem will rise and
> remain on its site from Benjamin's Gate as far as the place
> of the First Gate to the Corner Gate, and from the Tower
> of Hananel to the king's wine presses. And people will
> live in it, and there will be no more curse, for Jerusalem
> will dwell in security (Zechariah 14:9-11).

For the modern Jew who is looking for Messiah and the
rebuilding of the Third Temple, a problem surfaces as they read
in the Old Testament about the nature and scope of the Millennial

Temple. There is no way that such a structure will fit upon the current 35-acre Temple Mount. Thus, many have resolved the dilemma by settling for the dimensions of the previous two Temples, but attaching millennial meaning to the Third Temple.

Most Christians have no such problem, since they believe that there will be two more Temples. The next will be the short-lived Tribulation Temple that will be rebuilt upon the current Temple Mount after the Solomonic pattern. But the majority of Christians believe that a Fourth Temple will literally follow Ezekiel's dimensions and characteristics and will be erected and function for 1000 years during Christ's millennial rule.

20. Is the Millennial Temple eternal?

While the millennium and Millennial Temple will be a 1000-year warm-up for eternity, the Fourth Temple will not be eternal in scope. John notes some of the conditions of the eternal state when he wrote:

> And I saw a new heaven and a new earth; for the first heaven and the first earth passed away, and there is no longer any sea. And I saw the holy city, new Jerusalem, coming down out of heaven from God, made ready as a bride adorned for her husband. And I heard a loud voice from the throne, saying, "Behold, the tabernacle of God is among men, and He shall dwell among them, and they shall be His people, and God Himself shall be among them...." And I saw no temple in it, for the Lord God, the Almighty, and the Lamb, are its temple (Revelation 21:1-3,22).

Apparently a Temple will not be needed in eternity, since history will have come to an absolute end and the redeemed and damned will forever be separated. Sin will be totally abolished in all of its polluting aspects and, thus, there will be no need for a cleansed sanctuary in which a Holy God's presence can be established among sinful men. All believers will experience the eternally cleansing work of Christ in our resurrection bodies. For the first time, in eternity, believers will have direct access to God without the necessity of approaching Him through the shelter of Temple ritual.

P A R T   5

What Is the Significance of the Temples for Christians Today?

21. Why are Israel's past Temples important?

Israel's past Temples are important because they demonstrate, in history, God's gracious pursuit of mankind—even though we as sinners constantly do everything we can to avoid our holy God. The Tabernacle and past Temples demonstrate that sinful man is not forever cut off from his holy God, but that God can be approached through a single, righteous path that must meet His high standard of holiness. Such an illustration of God's requirement for fellowship with Him establishes His holiness and man's sin. Such realization prepares the way for that righteous standard that can be meet only through Jesus Christ—the "just and the justifier of the one who has faith in Jesus" (Romans 3:26).

22. What is the importance of the spiritual Temple?

Since a Temple is a dwelling place of God, whereby the omnipresent God of the Bible shows His favor upon a given people by associating His presence with them, the church and the individual believer in Christ is said to be a spiritual Temple of God in our current dispensation. During the church age, God does not project His glory and presence through a stone Temple, but through a living Temple made up of every member of the body of Christ. It is a special privilege that should serve as a motivation for godly living, to know that we are Christ's spiritual Temple.

23. What is the importance of the Tribulation Temple?

The Tribulation Temple is important because it is the Temple that many Jews in Israel are attempting to rebuild in our day. Knowing what the Bible teaches about past, present, and future Temples provides Christians with the needed framework for seeing the Third Temple from God's perspective. Even though Jewish expectations for their next Temple is that it will be the Messianic Temple, the Bible makes it clear that it will, instead, be the short-lived Antichrist Temple.

The fact that Israel has been reestablished as a nation since 1948, Jerusalem was recaptured in 1967, and an increasingly significant Jewish effort to rebuild the Third Temple is underway, tells us that we are approaching the end of the current church age and nearing the time of tribulation. God's end-time scenario is taking shape and focus upon a rebuilt Temple in Jerusalem is center stage. God's hand is at work.

24. What is the importance of the Millennial Temple?

The Millennial Temple shows us where history is moving. It is a testimony to what God has always intended His priestly nation—Israel—to be and how they should function. We see in the final Temple that God will always be a holy God and demand that those who associate with Him do so on the basis of absolute holiness. This can only be accomplished through the gracious work of Jesus Christ's atoning work on the cross.

As with all things future, the Millennial Temple gives us confidence that we can stand boldly for the truth in the dark days in which we currently live—knowing that God's plan is leading His people to victory.

Conclusion

There is in Jewish literature a saying that "the land of Israel is at the center of the world; Jerusalem is at the center of Israel; the Temple is at the center of Jerusalem."[43] Such ancient wisdom is very close to the biblical text and the prophetic plan of God. Israel, Jerusalem, and the Temple all have a unique role in the past, the present, and the future. The Temples of the past were magnificent and great; the Temples of the future will also be filled with splendor and riches. As important as the when, what, and where of the Tribulation and Millennial Temples are, it is even more important to keep our focus on the who of the Millennial Temple—our Lord Jesus Christ, "who is the blessed and only Sovereign, the King of kings and Lord of lords" (1 Timothy 6:15).

A Temple Chronology

c. 2000 B.C. Abraham and Isaac offer a ram on Mount Moriah

c. 1400 B.C. Moses describes service to be performed at the future central sanctuary (Temple)

996 B.C. David makes Jerusalem his capital and moves the Ark to a site adjacent to the Temple Mount

c. 990 B.C. David purchases the threshing floor of Araunah the Jebusite as the site for the First Temple

950 B.C. Solomon completes the First Temple

586 B.C. Babylonians destroy the Temple

515 B.C. Zerubbabel rebuilds the Temple

332 B.C. Alexander the Great conquers Jerusalem, but spares the Temple

169–167 B.C. Antiochus Epiphanes desecrates the Temple

20 B.C.–A.D. 64 Herod the Great remodels the Second Temple

c. A.D. 26–29 Jesus' ministry relates to the Temple

A.D. 70 Romans destroy the Temple

A.D. 132–135 Possible rebuilding of the Temple by Bar Kokhba

A.D. 363 Julian the Apostate attempts to rebuild the Temple; his effort fails

A.D. 443 Emperess Eudoxia permits a rebuilding of the Temple; the effort fails

A.D. 614 Persian effort to rebuild the Temple fails

A.D. 691 Moslems complete Dome of the Rock mosque on the Temple Mount

A.D. 1917 Jerusalem is conquered by the British

May 14, 1948 Israel becomes a nation

June 7, 1967 Israel recaptures the Temple Mount during the Six-Day War

June 17, 1967 Moshe Dayan returns the Temple Mount to the control of the Moslem Wakf

1967–present Jews struggle to rebuild the Third Temple[44]

Notes

1. Richard N. Ostling, "Time for a New Temple?" *Time* Magazine, October 16, 1989, pp. 64-65.
2. Gershon Salomon quoted in Patti Lalonde, "Building the Third Temple," *This Week in Bible Prophecy Magazine,* April 1995, p. 22.
3. Thomas S. McCall and Zola Levitt, *Satan in the Sanctuary* (Chicago: Moody Press, 1973), p. 33.
4. Thomas Ice and Randall Price, *Ready to Rebuild: The Imminent Plan to Rebuild the Last Days' Temple* (Eugene, OR: Harvest House Publishers, 1992), p. 43.
5. Ibid., pp. 41-42.
6. John F. Walvoord, *The Prophecy Knowledge Handbook* (Wheaton, IL: Victor Books, 1990), p. 257.
7. Tim LaHaye, *How to Study Bible Prophecy for Yourself* (Eugene, OR: Harvest House Publishers, 1990), p. 110.
8. Charles C. Ryrie, *The Ryrie Study Bible, New American Standard Translation* (Chicago: Moody Press, 1978), footnote for 2 Thessalonians 2:4.
9. Ice and Price, *Ready to Rebuild*, p. 55.
10. The Mishnah states that this rock had been at the site since the time of the early prophets (i.e., David and Solomon), and that it was three finger breadths higher than the ground (*Yoma* 5:2).
11. Midrash, *Radbaz*, Responsa, 2 (1882), nos. 639, 691.
12. Ice and Price, *Ready to Rebuild*, pp. 55, 57.
13. Talmud, *Succah* 51:b.
14. Ice and Price, *Ready to Rebuild*, p. 70.
15. Hal Lindsey, *There's a New World Coming* (Santa Ana, CA: Vision House Publishers, 1973), p. 160.
16. For a rebuttal of this viewpoint see H. Wayne House and Thomas Ice, *Dominion Theology: Blessing or Curse?* (Portland, OR: Multnomah Press, 1988), pp. 217-334.
17. John F. Walvoord, *Major Bible Prophecies: 37 Crucial Prophecies that Affect You Today* (Grand Rapids: Zondervan Publishing House, 1991), pp. 396, 397, 401-02.
18. Michael Avi-Yonah, *The Jews of Palestine* (Oxford: Basil Blackwell, 1976), p. 13.
19. Rabbi Leibel Reznick, *The Holy Temple Revisited* (Northvale, NJ: Jason Aronson, Inc., 1990), p. 156
20. *Paschal Chronicle* P.G. 92, 613; see also Benjamin Mazar, *The Mountain of the Lord* (New York: Doubleday and Co., 1975), p. 236.
21. For more details concerning efforts to rebuild the Temple see Ice and Price, *Ready to Rebuild*, pp. 25-38, 73-83.
22. Don Stewart and Chuck Missler, *The Coming Temple: Center Stage for the Final Countdown* (Orange, CA: Dart Press, 1991), pp. 84-85.
23. Ibid., p. 84.
24. *Jerusalem Post* (International edition), 12 August 1995. The incident reported in this issue is that of the detaining of 20 Jews who attempted to pray on the Temple Mount. It is not an unusual story, but rather typical of many stories which report the continued unrest on the Temple Mount.
25. For documented details of current preparations to rebuild the Temple see Ice and Price, *Ready to Rebuild*.
26. Randall Price taped interview with Gershon Salomon, June 24, 1991.
27. Ice and Price, *Ready to Rebuild*, pp. 173-74.
28. Ibid., p. 180.
29. For details about current activities by Jews in Israel to rebuild the Temple see Ice and Price, *Ready to Rebuild*, and Randall Price, *In Search of Temple Treasures* (Eugene, OR: Harvest House Publishers, 1994).
30. For more details and further rebuttal of this view see Ice and Price, *Ready to Rebuild*, pp. 154-58.
31. For a more extensive presentation and support of Kaufman's view see Stewart and Missler, *The Coming Temple*, pp. 145-56; and Hal Lindsey, *A Prophetical Walk Through the Holy Land* (Eugene, OR: Harvest House Publishers, 1983), pp. 57-75. A more extensive rebuttal of Kaufman's view see Ice and Price, *Ready to Rebuild*, pp. 158-63.

32. Randall Price taped interview with Dan Bahat, July 1991.
33. James DeYoung taped interview with Dan Bahat, July 1991.
34. Randall Price taped interview with Chaim Richmond, June 26, 1991.
35. Randall Price taped interview with Dan Bahat, July 1991.
36. For an overview of the many Jewish legends about finding the Ark of the Covenant see Price, *In Search of Temple Treasures*.
37. Price, *In Search of Temple Treasures*, pp. 32-33.
38. John F. Walvoord, *The Millennial Kingdom* (Findlay, OH: Dunham Publishing, 1959), pp. 310-11.
39. Jerry M. Hullinger, "The Problem of Animal Sacrifices in Ezekiel 40–48," *Bibliotheca Sacra* 152 (July-September 1995): 280.
40. Ibid., p. 281.
41. Ibid., p. 289.
42. Arnold G. Fruchtenbaum, *Israelology: The Missing Link in Systematic Theology* (Tustin, CA: Ariel Ministries Press, 1993), p. 810.
43. Midrash, *Tanhuma,* Kedoshim 10.
44. For a more detailed Temple chronology see Ice and Price, *Ready to Rebuild*, pp. 250-66.

Recommended Reading

Feinberg, Charles Lee. *The Prophecy of Ezekiel.* Chicago: Moody Press, 1969.

Fruchtenbaum, Arnold G. *The Footsteps of the Messiah.* Tustin, CA: Ariel Press, 1982.

_____. *Israelology: The Missing Link in Systematic Theology.* Tustin, CA: Ariel Press, 1993.

Hullinger, Jerry M. "The Problem of Animal Sacrifices in Ezekiel 40–48." *Bibliotheca Sacra* 152 (July–September 1995): 279-89.

Ice, Thomas and Price, Randall. *Ready to Rebuild.* Eugene, OR: Harvest House Publishers, 1992.

McCall, Thomas S., and Levitt, Zola, *Satan in the Sanctuary.* Chicago: Moody Press, 1973.

Pentecost, J. Dwight. *Things to Come.* Grand Rapids: Zondervan Publishing House, 1958.

Price, Randall. *In Search of Temple Treasures.* Eugene, OR: Harvest House Publishers, 1994.

Stewart, Don and Missler, Chuck. *The Coming Temple: Center Stage for the Final Countdown.* Orange, CA: Dart Press, 1991.

Walvoord, John F. *The Millennial Kingdom.* Findlay, OH: Dunham Publishing Co., 1958.

_____. *Major Bible Prophecies: 37 Crucial Prophecies that Affect You Today.* Grand Rapids: Zondervan Publishing House, 1991.